PARENTAL DIVORCE

Debra Goldentyer

CESAR CHAVEZ HIGH SCHOOL
8501 Howard
Houston, Texas 77017

RSVP
RAINTREE
STECK-VAUGHN
PUBLISHERS
The Steck-Vaughn Company

Austin, Texas

Consultants:
Beverly Arneth, Director, Family Guidance Center, Trenton, NJ
William B. Presnell, American Association for Marriage and Family Therapy

Developed for Steck-Vaughn Company by Visual Education Corporation, Princeton, New Jersey
Project Director: Paula McGuire
Editors: Jewel Moulthrop, Linda Perrin
Photo Research: Sara Matthews

Raintree Steck-Vaughn Publishers staff
Editor: Kathy Presnell
Project Manager: Julie Klaus
Electronic Production: Scott Melcer
Photo Editor: Margie Foster

Library of Congress Cataloging-in-Publication Data
Goldentyer Debra, 1960–
    Parental divorce / Debra Goldentyer.
        p.   cm. — (Teen hot line)
    Includes index.
    ISBN 0-8114-3817-1
    1. Children of divorced parents—Juvenile Literature. 2. Divorce—Juvenile Literature. [1. Divorce.] I. Title. II. Series.
    HQ777.5.G636   1995

                                                                94-32085
                                                                CIP
                                                                AC

Photo Credits: Cover: © Park Street; **14:** © Richard Hutchings/PhotoEdit; **21:** © David Young-Wolff/PhotoEdit; **29:** © PhotoEdit; **32:** © PhotoEdit; **44:** © Richard Hutchings/PhotoEdit; **53:** © Skjold Photographs; **56:** © Mary Kate Denny/PhotoEdit; **64:** © Michael Newman/PhotoEdit; **68:** © Mary Kate Denny/PhotoEdit; **72:** © Skjold Photographs; **74:** © PhotoEdit.

Printed and bound in the United States

1 2 3 4 5 6 7 8 9 0 LB 99 98 97 96 95

CONTENTS

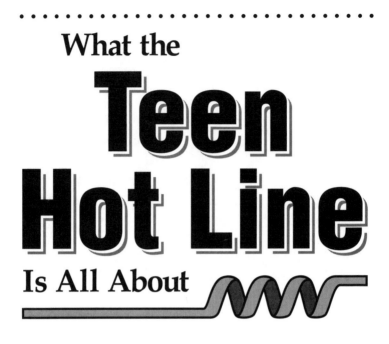

What the Teen Hot Line Is All About

This book is like a telephone hot line. It answers questions about parents' divorce that may be worrying you. Answering them requires us to give you the facts. You can use those facts to make your own decisions about what you're going to do about what's going on in your home. So think of us as the voice on the phone, always there to answer your questions, even the ones that are hard to ask.

Just so you know where we stand, we have made a list of steps that we think everybody should take when they find themselves facing their parents' divorce. We assume that you want to do what's best for you and for everyone in your family.

 Read books and call hot lines to find out what you need to know about parental divorce.

Talk to people you're close to—friends, teachers, other adults, and your parents—about what you're going through.

 Think about what's happening to you and what you want to do about it. Think about your options and how each option will affect those around you.

 Decide how you want to handle the situation.

5 Whatever you decide to do, take care of yourself. Keep in touch with how you feel, get counseling if you feel you need to, and join support groups to meet others who are going through situations like yours.

After you read this book, we hope that you will discover some answers to your questions and maybe to some you hadn't thought of yet. At the back of this book is a list of sources for further information. By thinking about the issues raised in this book, you will have made an important effort in taking control of your life.

Interview

Janice and Brian met in college. They married a few years later, went on to graduate schools, and began their careers. After six years of marriage, they had their first child, Carl. Their daughter, Laila, was born three years later. While their marriage started out strong and healthy, in time things began going wrong. Although no one story is typical, Janice's story includes a lot of the problems parents experience when they go through a divorce.

The problems were there practically since we met. I didn't know that then; it's only in looking back that I see what was wrong all along.

Eventually, what broke things down was that Brian was having an affair, which he didn't tell me about for two years. During that time, we had been going to counseling. So, when he finally did tell me, it felt like four betrayals on top of the initial one, in that we were going through counseling on totally false premises, because he was actually seeing this woman at that time.

One afternoon, he said he couldn't stand it anymore. It was too awful; it wasn't good for him to be somewhere where he wasn't wanted. At that point, it had been nine months since I'd found out about the affair, and the counseling wasn't working. It was a huge relief; I wouldn't have to struggle with the issue anymore.

We sat the kids down. We told them, "You're going to

be fine, we both have jobs, we don't plan to change your schools, and you're our primary interest." It was a blow, but they knew things had been pretty bad. They didn't say anything. They just sat there, wide-eyed and hurt, bewildered, worrying about what was going to happen.

As time went on, the kids were so confused that they didn't know what to say or do. Carl's grades went down. Laila became extremely clingy. She'd hang on me like a monkey; Brian would have to pull her off when it was time to take her. He lived right around the corner, which was quite convenient.

Brian and I still had to settle matters, so we started working with a mediator, but Brian couldn't handle it. We'd settle something, and he'd just reopen it the next week. It was terrible.

He started making ugly threats. He'd say, "You can't do it on your own; I'm not going to pay a penny. I'll take the kids, I have the money, I can take care of the kids better than you can." Because my self-esteem at that point was so low, I assumed, of course, that he was right. I would assume that they didn't love me—of course they'd go with him. Who wouldn't? He's got more goodies than I have.

I wanted to be a major figure in my kids' life, and the notion that he would somehow take them away from me was really frightening. As far as I knew, I was going to be living in a trailer somewhere out in the sticks—financially, I didn't know how I could survive on my income. He was just as punitive and awful as he could be.

Eventually, we each ended up with an attorney. My attorney said, "Wait a minute. He can't take the kids from you. Even if you went to prison, you'd still get partial custody of your children." The custody decisions are made before financial decisions, and they're not based on who has more money. That was really reassuring. It made me realize I would be able to survive and keep contact with the children.

When we first separated, Brian made a few contacts with Carl, but he didn't make any contact with Laila for nearly six weeks. And then he did take her, but he had her stay overnight with the neighbors who had a couple of little girls.

Laila counted that as a visit with Daddy, but he just didn't seem to be able to do anything with her, take her to a park or anything. My attorney said, with that kind of record, he'd have an impossible time trying to demonstrate that he truly wanted to be the main parent in his kids' lives.

Making a home for them or finding time for them—he just couldn't do any of that. But he wanted some contact with the children. At first, he really felt he couldn't handle both kids at the same time. So he had one visit with Carl for a weekend, then a weekend off, then a visit with Laila. Gradually, he added more visits. The schedule we've had now for some time is, out of a four-weekend month, both kids are with me one weekend, both kids are with him one weekend. One kid's with him one weekend and me the other, and one's with me the other weekend and him the other. We each get one weekend off, and we get one weekend with both kids. They also go over there Wednesday nights for dinner, and often one of them stays overnight.

It's been four years now since we separated. Laila went through a period when she'd say, "Oh, goody, I get to go to Daddy's." Just last year it became, "Oh, my weekend over there," and then she'd sigh. Now it's, "Mommy, I don't want to go—do I have to go?"

Carl hasn't had any luck getting his father to improve his relationship with him. And I've got to stay out of it; he's their father. I've never had any luck getting him to do what I wanted—I certainly wouldn't have any luck getting him to do what they wanted.

My relationship with Brian is uncomfortable. We exchange information about the kids. I see him a couple of times a week, when I pick Laila up or drop her off. And we talk a couple of times a week—about the school open house, a birthday party, or a child having trouble in class. Carl had a car accident a few weeks ago, and there's always something that needs to be clarified or explained, things like that.

Brian is now living with his girlfriend. She doesn't try to mother the kids at all. She and Laila ride horses together. She doesn't have a lot of contact with Carl. I mean, they talk at the dinner table and so on, but she doesn't seem to be a major player in his life. It would be OK either way.

I've only had a couple of dates since the divorce. I

think the kids like the notion of my dating. They're protective of me, and they'd like for me to have some fun. I can't imagine letting a man into my life who didn't accept them—if not love them and think they're wonderful—or at least leave lots of room in my life for me to be their mother.

I see a lot of children struggling with their parents' divorce. They need to ask for help. I don't think a lot of kids think the divorce is their fault—I think kids are more savvy than that—but they need to realize that they are really wounded, that they are hurt. They are hurt by the family relationship before the divorce, by what's going on during the divorce, and by what goes on right after. They need to get help from school counseling or outside counseling or support groups. We all tend to think we're alone and we're the crazy ones. Even when we're told we're not crazy, we don't believe it. Working with other people can help us understand that. This is particularly important for teenagers, who are trying to figure out who they are in the world, trying to go to school, and having to deal with a miserable family life all at the same time.

BULLETIN BOARD

Number of married Americans: 113.3 million (61.1% of the population 18 years old and over)

Number of divorced Americans: 16.3 million (8.8% of the population 18 years old and over)

Number of married couples with own children under 18: 24.5 million (25.5% of all households)

Number of single men living with children: 3 million (3% of all households)

Number of single women living with children: 7 million (7% of all households)

Number of marriages per year: 2.4 million

Number of divorces per year: 1.2 million

Percentage of marriages that are first marriages for both the man and the woman: 54%

Percentage of marriages that are remarriages for both: 23%

Median age of the first marriage for women and for men: 24 and 26

Median age of divorce for women and for men: 33 and 35

Median age of remarriage for women and for men: 34 and 37

Median duration of marriage: 7 years

Number of children under 18 whose parents get divorced: 1 million (16 per 1,000)

Percentage of divorces that involve children: over 70%

Percentage of all divorces that are sought by women: 72%

Percentage of divorced people who remarry: 80%

Percentage of women who receive alimony after a divorce: 10-15%

Percentage of men who are granted sole custody of their children after divorce: 10%

Standard of living for a woman after divorce: down 70%

Standard of living for a man after divorce: up 40%

Statistical Abstract of the United States, 1993: The National Data Book. U.S. Department of Commerce, Bureau of the Census.

CHAPTER 1

Communicating

Q My parents fight all the time. I think they're talking about getting a divorce, but no one's talked to me about it. Don't I have a right to know what's going on?

A Yes, you do have a right to know what's going on in your family. The truth is, though, your parents may not yet know themselves what's going on. Most couples find it very hard to decide whether it would be better to get a divorce or to try staying together. All couples have troubles now and then, but not all troubles lead to divorce. It may be that your parents are still thinking about whether a divorce makes sense for them. It may be that the troubles they're having are just temporary.

• • • • • • • • • • • •

Q But the other day, I heard Mom talking to her friend. She said they're splitting up.

A It may be that they are. Or it may be that your mother was just particularly upset during that conversation. Most couples fluctuate a lot before deciding whether to go through with a divorce. And many "split up"—have a trial separation—before going through with anything permanent.

• • • • • • • • • • • •

It is difficult for children to witness any angry scene involving their parents, especially if such scenes are repeated often. The children worry and want to know whether or not the trouble between their parents is serious.

 Well, I don't want them to get divorced.

A Most young people would prefer that their parents stay together. But if they really are arguing all the time, it might be best for them—and for you—if they were to live separately. Children whose parents have divorced often find that it's much better to live with one happy parent than to live with two fighting parents.

• • • • • • • • • • •

Q Why haven't they talked to me about all this?

A One reason may be that they haven't yet decided what to do. They don't want to talk to you about it because they don't know what to say. They can't say whether they will divorce. They can't tell you where things will be in six months or a year. They may figure it's best to wait until they know something and can give you the whole story.

Even if they have decided to divorce, it's possible that they're waiting for the right opportunity to tell you. They may want to work out the details, such as who's going to move out and where it's best for you to live. Or they may be ready to tell you but are too scared, upset, or angry to discuss it calmly.

. . . .

Q But I want to know now.

A It may sound odd, but if your parents aren't saying anything, they're probably being quiet for your protection. They know that a divorce would not be good news to you. They don't want to upset or worry you.

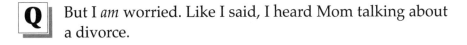

Q But I *am* worried. Like I said, I heard Mom talking about a divorce.

A Then maybe it's time you brought it up with your parents. Although they may mean well by being silent, they obviously aren't keeping you from worrying. If you tell them how you're feeling, perhaps they can tell you what's going on. Remember, though, they can't tell you what they don't know themselves.

Keep in mind, if you can, that this may be a very difficult time for your parents. Be patient with your parents. If you're a family, you need to support each other in whatever ways you can.

• • • • • • • • • • • •

Making Your Decision

"Divorce" may be a very frightening word to you. If what's going on between your parents is keeping you awake at night, it may be time to talk with them. If you're not sure whether you want to talk to your parents about what's going on, you might want to start by learning more about divorce. Once you understand more about the issues involved, you might worry a little less.

■ First, examine the facts. What are your parents going through right now? What are the possible outcomes? What would be the worst that could happen if they did divorce?

■ Second, examine your feelings. Now that you know a few facts about divorce, what do you think would be best—for your parents to stay together and be unhappy or for them to separate? Would it be best for you to know now what's going on between your parents, or would you rather wait until they can give you the whole story? Which would worry you less? Do you think they're ready to talk to you? Think about what their answers might be—are you prepared to hear them now?

■ Finally, make your decision about whether or not it's time to talk to them.

Communicating About the Problem

Making the decision to talk about what's going on is hard, but actually having the conversation will be hard, too. Let's say you decide you need to talk about the possibility of a divorce. Planning ahead for the conversation might make having it a little easier.

Planning the Conversation

What makes the most sense—to talk to your mother and father together or to talk to each one separately? When would be the best time to talk? Do you want to set up a time to talk or just catch them during a quiet time?

Some people find it hard to say certain things aloud, no matter how many times they've rehearsed them in their heads. If that's true for you, you might want to practice your conversation with a friend. Role-play; pretend the friend is your mother or father and try out the conversation.

Having the Conversation

As you begin the conversation, remember how hard it may be for your parents to talk about this. You may want to reassure them that you know they want to do what's best for you. You may also want to remind them that it's important to you that they be truthful. Tell them that you've thought about it and you'd rather know what they know now than wait until they are sure what's going to happen. At the same time, you must be honest with them.

Chances are, during your conversation, your parents may say that nothing that happens is your fault, that they both still love you as much as they always have, and that the problems between them are only between them. Stop and listen to those words. You may doubt some of them at first, but let the words sink in.

Remember that the conversation may be difficult at times. Your parents may get upset. You may get upset. You may hear things you wish weren't true. But remember how much thought you put into whether you wanted this conversation and remember why you felt it was important.

Keeping Lines of Communication Open

Your conversation probably won't make things better. If your parents are having problems, the problems may continue for a while. Whether or not they get a divorce, your parents have a lot of things to sort out.

In time, things will settle down. During the interim, try to keep the lines of communication open. Ask your parents if they will keep you up-to-date on what they decide. Ask them if you can talk to them when you get upset. Let them know if things get too hard for you at home. It might make sense for you to see a counselor to help get through the hard times.

No matter how you decide to handle yourself during these hard times at home, making important decisions on your own and taking care of yourself are the first steps toward taking control of your life.

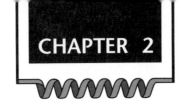

CHAPTER 2

Why Parents Divorce

Q My name's Glenn. My parents told me last night that they're getting a divorce. This just came out of the blue. How can they make a decision like this all at once?

A Chances are, they didn't make this decision all at once. If your parents are like most divorcing couples, there have been problems between them for a while. They have probably been thinking about this divorce for quite some time. They just weren't ready to tell you about it until now, most likely because they weren't sure it was really going to happen. Many couples talk about splitting up, then decide they'd rather stay together. If your parents had told you earlier they were breaking up and then they decided not to, they might have gotten you upset for no reason.

• • • • • • • • • • •

The decision to divorce rarely pops out of nowhere. Couples usually come to it gradually. Most of the time, it takes months or years for a couple to realize that what they're going through isn't a "phase" or something that will go away. It takes that long for them to realize that the relationship is over and that it doesn't make sense to live together anymore.

You may have noticed some signs that there was trouble. Think back to what's been going on in your home lately. Have your parents appeared to be upset or troubled? Has it felt as if there's a great deal of stress hanging over everything? Can you remember any fighting, crying, or long silences? Has either parent been staying away from home? Have things just "felt different" around the house? All of these are signs that there may have been trouble for a while.

If your parents have decided to get a divorce, there's very little you can do about it. It's between them. Their divorce will affect you as much as it does them, but it has nothing to do with how either one feels about you.

You'll have a lot to get used to over the next year or so. You're probably feeling very scared. It may be hard to believe right now, but things will settle down. Your family may even be happier in the end.

Why Couples Divorce

Rupert and Lisbeth met in high school. They got married right after graduation. They were both 18 years old; they adored each other. It was the perfect marriage, they thought.

As time moved on, things became less perfect. Rupert and Lisbeth developed different interests. They had different friends and spent their time doing different things. They disagreed about many things, such as where to live and what sort of house to buy. When their son, Daryl, was born, they both enjoyed spending time with him and with each other, but that didn't last. As with everything else, they had different ideas about how to raise Daryl.

It got to the point that the only time Rupert and Lisbeth talked was when they talked about Daryl. But every time they talked about Daryl, they fought. Both grew to dread the times they spent alone together. By the time Daryl was ten years old, Rupert and Lisbeth had nothing in common. The 30-year-olds they had become were not in love like the teenagers they had once been. They didn't even like each other very much. It wasn't too much later that they decided to get a divorce.

There are many reasons why people get divorced. Some couples, like Rupert and Lisbeth, marry young and begin to change as they grow older. They drift apart, or they find they can't get along. Some couples marry too soon after they meet, before they know each other very well. Then they find out later that they aren't really compatible. They may find they have too many different ideas and don't enjoy each other's company.

Some marriages fall apart when one partner falls out of love with the other or falls in love with someone else. Sometimes one partner has personal problems, such as mental illness, addictions, or compulsive behaviors that tear the two apart. Sometimes a couple has sexual differences or difficulties. Sometimes one partner deserts the family. Sometimes one partner abuses the other or the children.

When a couple breaks up, one or both of the partners may spend a lot of time and energy trying to figure out whose fault it is. The truth is, it doesn't really matter. Placing blame doesn't make the problem go away and doesn't stop the divorce from happening. It only makes getting over it more difficult.

Making the Decision

The decision to divorce is usually very hard to make. Most married people are afraid of

Some divorcing parents are upset and cannot bear to face their children. If a parent leaves the home without any explanation, his or her children may be hurt, bewildered, and angry.

divorce. When they got married, they envisioned a lifelong, loving relationship and an intact, happy family. A divorce ends all of that.

People deciding to divorce have a lot of mixed feelings. They worry about what the divorce will do to them, to their spouses, and, most of all, to their children. They worry about how they will support themselves, where they will live, where the children will live, and whether they'll ever get married again. On top of that, they're often angry, too, at themselves and at the other person. Some are also ashamed of or embarrassed by their decision. Most of all, they're probably frightened.

Because it's such a hard decision, many couples start with a trial separation before they decide to divorce. In a trial separation, one partner moves out of the house for a while so both can see what it would be like if they separated permanently. Some couples discover that splitting up would be a terrible mistake, while others find that although living separately is very hard at times, it makes for a much happier life in the end.

Living with Unhappy Parents

Glenn's parents kept their problems well hidden. He didn't know there was anything wrong until the day they announced their divorce.

Not all young people have that experience. Many parents don't keep their troubles to themselves. Some try but don't succeed. Their children hear fighting behind closed doors. They see parents with red eyes after an argument. They hear long silences where there once was conversation. They notice their parents not talking to each other, leaving the table in the middle of a meal, or not showing up for meals at all. They can feel the tension in the air.

Other parents don't try to keep their troubles from their children. Some may talk to their children about what's going on. Sometimes this helps the children adjust to the idea. Often, however, it only upsets or scares the children even more.

This is especially true when one or both parents try to get the children to take sides. Mona's dad hardly ever ate dinner with the family anymore. Whenever Mona asked her mother where he was, her mother would answer, "He's probably off with one of his girlfriends," or "He could be dead in the street for all I care." Mona didn't know what was or was not true; she only knew that she hated hearing her mother talk about her father like that.

Some parents, because they are immature, troubled, and self-ish, may even openly blame their teenage children for "causing" the marital split. Over the years the existence of the children may have been interpreted as interfering with one or both of the parents' freedom to live as they wanted. They decide the marriage is over and place the burden of guilt on the children. Knowing how their parents feel about them, such children may be left with serious emotional damage. They may need help to overcome a feeling of responsibility for their parents' divorce. They may also need help to overcome feelings of rejection and alienation in order to be able to have loving relationships in the future.

Trying to Work It Out
Some couples work out their differences on their own. Others choose to get marriage counseling or therapy when they have troubles. By talking out their problems with a counselor, a couple can often see more clearly what is going on and whether things can be fixed.

Many couples find that even if counseling doesn't stop a divorce, it helps in a number of other ways. A counselor can help the partners work out their anger safely, so they don't take it out on each other or on the children. A counselor can help make the transition from marriage to divorce easier on both the partners and on the children. People who are constantly fighting or who refuse to speak to each other can't settle the many issues that come up during a divorce. A counselor can help people work out those issues in a cooperative manner.

Staying Together for the Children

After ten years of marriage, Wayne and Maria found that they didn't love each other anymore. Both wanted a divorce. But they had three children whom they loved more than anything in the world. Wayne and Maria agreed that it was important to do whatever was best for the children.

After much discussion, Wayne and Maria decided to stay together for the sake of the children. They figured they could

Families with Children
Number and Percentage of Families with Own Children
under 18 Years Old, by Family Type: 1950 to 1990

(Numbers in thousands)

Families with own[1] children under 18

Year	Total Families	Number	Percent of Total Families	Married-Couple Families	Single-Parent Families
1950	39,193	20,267	51.7	47.9	3.8
1960	45,062	25,662	56.9	51.8	5.2
1970	51,237	28,666	55.9	49.6	6.4
1980	58,426	30,517	52.2	42.0	10.2
1990	66,090	32,289	48.9	37.1	11.7

[1] "Own" children in a family are sons and daughters, including stepchildren and adopted children, of the householder.
Source: Bureau of the Census

get a divorce ten years later, when all three children were grown and out of the house.

Many parents make the decision to stay married, hoping to protect their children from the difficulties of divorce. Sometimes it's the best decision they can make. Many times, however, it's the worst.

It can be the worst decision because it doesn't settle any differences. If a couple is having problems, those problems are not likely to go away by themselves. If they aren't settled, the fights, the long silences, the long absences, the tension, and the unhappiness will still be there. No matter how hard parents try to hide their unhappiness, their children can sense it.

Living in a tense or unhappy home can make a child feel anxious and worried. Children of miserable parents don't know whether the fighting will ever stop or whether it will get worse. Often these children secretly welcome a divorce. If their parents would just get it over with, these children think, they could all get on with their lives.

There is often another problem when parents stay together for the children's sake. The children understand that their parents are making a great sacrifice for them. As a result, they feel a tremendous amount of guilt and responsibility. When they get older, they may find it hard to go off to college or get an apartment of their own. Knowing that their parents will divorce as soon as they leave, they feel that they must stay at home to keep their parents together.

Sometimes, if a couple can find a way to stay together without too many problems, it's best for the children. It lets the children grow up with the support of both parents in one home. However, many people who grew up with parents who stayed together just for their sake often say that divorce would have been the better option. If their parents had divorced, they might not have felt all that stress and tension while growing up. They would not have experienced the sadness of their parents, and the guilt that they now feel.

Telling You

Many parents say the hardest thing about divorcing is how it will affect their children. Since it's such bad news, parents are never sure of the best way to tell their children that they're getting a divorce. In order to protect their children, many keep quiet about the problems for as long as possible. Some tell their children only after the decision to divorce has been made.

Some parents never tell their children at all. Mike's father simply moved out one day. Mike asked his mother what was going on; only then did she tell him that they were getting a divorce. It was quite a shock to Mike. He was upset about the news. Even more, he was angry at his father for walking out without saying a word. His father may have chosen to do this because he couldn't stand to see Mike upset. Maybe he was afraid to say the word "divorce" out loud because doing so would make it feel real and final. He may have felt ashamed and been afraid that Mike would think his father had let him down. He may have been too angry about what was going on between him and Mike's mother to be able to talk about it calmly.

Unfortunately, there's no way for a parent to make the announcement of a divorce painless for the children. Divorce is always a hard thing to talk about.

However, to a young person living in a house full of angry silences or, conversely, the noise of slammed doors, screaming, and tears, the word "divorce" sometimes comes as a relief. Only after the divorce begins can things change. Only after the decision is made can the family move on to a better life.

CHAPTER 3

Reacting to the Divorce

Q My name is Barry, and my parents argue all the time about money. Now they say they're getting a divorce. Will it help if I get a job after school? If I help out financially, they'll have less reason to fight over money, and maybe they'll change their minds about splitting up.

A Getting a job won't help. In fact, chances are there's nothing you can do to stop your parents' divorce. In most cases, people don't get divorced because of simple things like money. The fights over money are just a sign of deeper problems with their marriage. Even if you could solve the financial problems, the more serious problems would remain.

• • • • • • • • • • • •

Your getting a job might even add to your parents' problems. If you get a job, your life will be harder because you'll have less time to spend on schoolwork, less time for friends, and less energy to help out at home. When your parents see that you're making such a difficult sacrifice, each may blame the other for putting you in that position.

While there's probably nothing you can do to stop the divorce, there's a lot you can do to make it easier on yourself. Don't take your parents' problems onto your shoulders. Work on maintaining your own mental health.

Remember that your parents still love you, even if they have stopped loving each other. Neither one wants to hurt you. If they're doing things that are bothering you, let them know. They probably won't call off the divorce, but they may be able to handle it in a way that causes you less pain.

In fact, even though it may not seem true right now, one of the reasons your parents are divorcing is to make your life better. They know that in the long run, you'll be happier living with one parent than living in a family where people are fighting all the time.

How It Feels When Parents Split Up

Everyone reacts differently to the news of their parents' divorce. Some people cry. Others shout at their parents. Others say nothing at first, maybe because they're too angry or too stunned to react at all. Many people go through a number of reactions. They may at first be stunned, like Joe; then they may become angry, resentful, or upset.

If your parents are divorcing, you no doubt have strong feelings of your own. These feelings are not unusual, and they should be accepted as a valid response to the situation. However, they may hinder your work or your daily activities. If you're not comfortable with the way you're feeling, you might want to talk with a supportive adult. Try talking to a counselor, an adult friend, a grandparent, or a favorite aunt or uncle. It can be very beneficial to talk to someone who is outside of the immediate family, someone not directly involved in the home situation.

The Stages of Adjustment

When confronted with upsetting news, most people go through several emotional stages. No matter what kind of news it is—a divorce, an illness in the family, a death, or another serious event—the emotional stages are usually the same. These stages are *denial, anger, fear, grieving,* and *acceptance.*

Denial

Even if they think they "saw it coming" for some time, some young people aren't ready to hear that their parents are about to divorce. Because news of the breakup is hard to accept, they deny it—that is, they decide not to accept it. They think that they can wish it away. They tell themselves that what's happening isn't happening, and they ignore all evidence that the divorce is real.

That's how it was for Tess. Tess's parents told her they were splitting up, and her father moved out of their home. For weeks afterward, she waited patiently for him to come back. Every evening, she'd set a place at the dinner table for him. Whenever she heard someone at their door, she assumed it would be her father.

Tess was in denial about her parents' divorce. It took more than a month for her to overcome these feelings. Finally, the truth began to sink in. Tess was ready to admit to herself that her father would not be coming home again.

Anger

When their parents split up, most young people feel anger. They get angry at their parents, at the situation, or at the world. Along with the anger comes frustration. They say to themselves, "Why me? What did I do to deserve this?"

If you hear that your parents are divorcing, you will undoubtedly have strong feelings of sadness and loss. You will need time to adjust to the new situation.

These feelings of anger and frustration are perfectly natural and appropriate. After all, if your parents decide to get a divorce, they're not going to ask for your permission first. It's an event that will affect your entire life, and you can't do anything to stop it. All you can do is get angry.

Grace was furious at her parents when they told her they'd decided to divorce. She felt that they hadn't really tried to save their marriage. After her mother moved out, she refused to speak to her father. When her father asked if anything was wrong, Grace said no.

Deep inside, Grace felt guilty about how she was treating her father. She knew that he was trying hard to make things OK and that he wasn't trying to hurt her. Emotionally, however, she couldn't stop the anger she felt.

If you feel the way Grace did, don't keep your feelings bottled up. Let yourself feel the anger. As time passes, you'll feel it less and less.

Fear

Once they know that their parents really are going to split up, many young people begin to feel afraid. They worry about all the immediate changes that will take place: Who will move out? Where will everyone live? What will the legal process be like? How difficult will the adjustment be?

They may also worry about the future: How will they survive without the constant contact with both parents? How will they get by financially when the parents live apart? How long will it take until everything feels normal?

In addition to these worries about practical matters, there are also more abstract fears. No matter how many times they're told the divorce is not their fault, many young people continue to feel partly responsible. They may fear that one or both of their parents will stop loving them or will abandon them.

These fears may linger for quite a long time. They may make it difficult to deal with other problems that come up in day-today life. For a teenager whose life is already so full of difficult questions, the unknowns stemming from a divorce can become overwhelming.

Grieving

Once it becomes clear that their parents' marriage is over, many young people go through a period of grieving. They feel a deep sadness, like the sadness they'd feel if someone close to them had died.

In a way, a divorce is very much like a death. When your parents divorce, you lose the family life you've been used to. Grieving is an important step in accepting that loss.

Acceptance

If you only just heard about your parents' plans to divorce, you may not believe that you'll ever accept the news. But after enough time has passed, you almost certainly will.

Accepting the situation doesn't necessarily mean liking it. It means adjusting to your new life and making the best of it. It means feeling "normal" again.

Over time, some of your anger will diminish, and some of your fears will be put to rest. You'll get used to your new living arrangement. You'll find that you can concentrate on things besides the divorce. You'll find that you can have a stable home life that's comfortable and loving—even if it's different from the one you were used to.

Other Feelings

Even after you've accepted the truth of your parents' divorce, you'll probably experience many different feelings. You may become depressed or feel ashamed. You may feel as if you've been abandoned. You may be lonely. You may remain angry or afraid. You may feel several of these emotions all at once.

This kind of emotional confusion is common among teens

whose parents get divorced. Remember that there's nothing wrong with what you're feeling—your mixed emotions are a natural response to a difficult situation. If you remain aware of what you're feeling and why you're feeling it, you may get through the situation a little more easily.

Shame

When his father moved out of the house, Tony was embarrassed and ashamed. He didn't want anyone to know that his parents had split up. He thought it made him look bad, so he tried to hide it. He stopped inviting friends over to his house. He made up stories about things he and his parents were doing together. He never said a word about the breakup, even to his best friend.

Tony knew he couldn't keep the divorce a secret forever. He worked hard to invent reasons for the divorce that others

If you continue to feel depressed, don't keep your feelings to yourself. Try talking to your brother or sister or a good friend. If necessary, seek out a counselor who is trained to give you support and sort out your feelings.

would accept. Finally, he told his friends that his father needed to take a job in a different city. He said that he and his mother were staying here so that Tony could finish school.

Tony spent so much time inventing stories that he made life much more difficult for himself. He spent less time than he wanted with his friends. He felt dishonest. And, worst of all, he couldn't tell his best friend how he was really feeling about what was happening at home.

There's nothing to be ashamed of when your parents divorce. Everyone understands that your parents' behavior has nothing to do with you. Your friends like you for who *you* are; what happens between your parents shouldn't affect your friendships in any way.

Your friends want to help you get through the hard parts of the divorce, if you'd only allow them to do so. And chances are they can offer a great deal of help. Any burden is lighter when it's shared.

Abandonment
When one of your parents moves out of the house, you're likely to feel abandoned. You may feel that the departing parent no longer loves you or cares about you. Even if you didn't have a close relationship with that parent, you may still feel abandoned, because now it is less likely that the two of you will ever have a chance to get close.

Many young people feel abandoned by both parents, even if only one has moved out. Flora, for instance, had always depended on her mom for help with schoolwork and working out practical problems. Her dad was her best friend and confidant—he helped her whenever she had boyfriend or girlfriend troubles or just needed to talk. When her parents separated, Flora lost the constant support that she had come to depend on. She had to seek out help from one parent or the other, instead of having both there when she needed them.

If you find yourself in this situation, look for support from someone outside the family. And remember that this period of turmoil won't last forever. After the divorce is settled, your parents will once again be there for you when you need them.

Physical Reactions
Your parents' divorce changes your life in many ways. In addition to the emotional reactions, you may have some physical reactions to the news. Some teens reexperience problems they had when they were much younger—for example, wetting their beds, having nightmares, or being afraid of the dark. Some literally cling to their parents or constantly ask for hugs and reassurances. Psychologists say that these reactions are a subconscious way to go back to the happier days of childhood.

You may feel sick to your stomach or have more headaches than before. All of these are normal reactions to the tension you're feeling. You can minimize your physical reactions to the tension in your life by taking good care of yourself. Try to eat healthy meals and get plenty of rest.

Dealing with Your Feelings

As your parents' divorce goes on, you'll find yourself having lots of strong feelings. Living with all those feelings can be difficult. You may want to try to ignore them and go on living as if everything were normal.

But ignoring your feelings is never a good idea. They'll still be there, whether or not you pay attention to them. They may pop up years later and in unexpected ways. You may have trouble forming loving relationships with people. You may even develop stress-related physical symptoms, such as ulcers or heart disease.

Find a healthy way to deal with your feelings now. If necessary, get professional help from a counselor or a doctor. By taking care of yourself now, you can lessen the problems you may have later.

Withdrawing

Many young people react to their parents' divorce by withdrawing from the world. They stop talking to friends, stop engaging in social activities, and sit quietly by themselves at school. They refuse to talk about how they feel. If anyone asks them, they say there's nothing wrong.

Withdrawal is often accompanied by depression. Depressed people feel empty and unhappy. Things that usually make them happy no longer do. Depressed people often have sleeping problems or eating problems. They may sleep too much or find they can't get to sleep. They may overeat or else have no appetite at all. Depressed teens don't feel like doing things with their friends or parents. They often feel very lonely, even when they're in a room full of people.

But even if you're feeling depressed, withdrawing isn't a good thing to do. Holding your feelings inside can make your problems worse. It also makes things worse for your family, because if you insist that there's nothing wrong, no one can really help you.

Acting Out

Some young people *do* express their feelings, but toward the wrong people. For example, when Lily's parents divorced, she took her frustration out on her best friend, Clarice. If Clarice was five minutes late or forgot to call when she promised she would, Lily would scream at her. Lily wasn't really angry at Clarice—she was angry at her parents for splitting up. But Clarice was the one who suffered.

Other young people take their anger out on themselves. They drop out of school, run away, or use drugs or alcohol. Some misbehave in class to get the attention they feel they're lacking at home. Others join gangs, shoplift, vandalize, or commit other crimes. Subconsciously, they may feel that doing these things will make their parents pay more attention to them.

Such self-destructive behavior helps no one. You're much

better off finding healthy ways to let your bad feelings out. For example, talk directly to the people involved: tell your parents just how you feel about their divorce. If that's not possible, go to a quiet place and cry or beat on a pillow. Some young people take up sports or other extracurricular activities to reduce the stress of problems at home. Acting on your feelings won't make them go away, but it may make them easier to handle.

Fixing Things

Because a divorce is not the children's fault, the children can't do anything to stop it. Nevertheless, many young people try various ways to stop the divorce anyway.

Some children beg and plead for their parents to stay together. Others, like Barry, look for problems within the marriage and try to fix them. Barry tried to solve his parents' financial problems. In the same way, some young people start helping with household chores or keeping peace with their brothers and sisters. They figure that their parents will have a better chance of working out their differences if they don't have to worry about the children.

Parenting

Some people say that their parents' divorce made adults out of them. With only one parent in the house, they were expected to take on more adult responsibilities, such as household chores and babysitting. Often, teenagers in single-parent homes are required to get jobs to help support a financially strapped family.

Some children of divorcing parents find that they become emotionally more mature as well. Especially if a parent is having a hard time going through the divorce, his or her child may become almost like a parent to that parent. Some teenagers say that they found themselves putting their parents' needs before their own for the first time in their lives. For example, they may go out with friends less often because they know how lonely their parent gets at home alone.

CHAPTER 4

The Legal Process

Q My parents are splitting up. There are lots of details they have to work out, but they're both too angry. I wish they'd get this over with. But how can they settle everything when they're not even talking to each other?

A It may take some time, and it probably will be difficult. Now that your parents have decided to get a divorce, they have many more decisions to make. They have to divide their possessions and sort out many financial matters. They have to decide where they're going to live and where you're going to live. The sooner all these matters are settled, the sooner all of you can begin your new lives.

• • • • • • • • • • • •

Your parents are facing the same problems all divorcing couples face. They're probably experiencing a mixture of unpleasant feelings. They may be upset, angry, depressed, scared, and worried. They may feel rejected or lonely, even if they are still living together. They may even hate each other. Most of these feelings will lessen in time. But right now, these feelings are making it hard for your parents to sit down and work things out.

One thing that might help is for your parents to spend some time away from each other. In fact, many states require a couple to separate for a while before they are permitted to divorce. Living apart gives the couple a chance to "cool down," get used to the new situation, and think about what they want for the future. After six months or a year, they'll be better prepared to make sensible decisions about themselves and about you.

Even after the separation, it may be hard for your parents to make these decisions. They may decide to hire lawyers or a mediator to help them work some things out. If they still can't come to an agreement, they may take the matter to a family court. There, a judge will review the family's situation and make the decisions for them.

Divorce and the Law

Like other difficult situations, a divorce is easier to get through when you understand what's going on. Let's take a brief look at the legal side of divorce, so you'll know what to expect if it happens in your own family.

Marriage means different things to different people. For some it is a public expression of love; for others it is a religious or spiritual act. In all cases, however, marriage is also a legal contract. When two people get married, they take on certain responsibilities. Those responsibilities include providing for each other financially, filling each other's emotional needs, and caring for any children they might have.

The only way to end the contract is to get a divorce. A divorce is a legal process in which the partners divide the responsibilities they took on when they got married. They must do this in a way that is fair to everyone involved, including the children.

Fault or No-Fault

It used to be that a couple had to have "grounds for divorce." That is, they could only get a divorce if one partner could convince a judge that the other had done something wrong. Grounds for divorce included adultery, desertion, mental or physical cruelty, or drug addiction.

Now, all states offer what is called a "no-fault" divorce. If both partners agree that they can no longer get along, a judge will grant them a divorce. Neither partner needs to prove that the other is to blame.

The Judge

Most of the time, both partners agree that they want to get divorced. They also usually agree on what to do about their children, finances, and property. Once they've worked out all the details, the couple submits their plan to a family court judge. If the plan appears fair, the judge grants the divorce. This is called an uncontested divorce. These days, most divorces are uncontested.

Sometimes, however, the couple cannot easily reach an agreement. In some cases, only one partner wants to get divorced. In other cases, both partners agree to get divorced, but they can't agree on a divorce settlement. A divorce in which the partners disagree is called a contested divorce.

A contested divorce requires a court trial. During the trial, each partner presents his or her side of the disagreement. A divorce trial has no jury. It is up to the judge to listen to both sides and come up with a fair settlement.

Lawyers

In most divorces, even uncontested divorces, each partner hires a lawyer. This is true even when the partners are getting along relatively well. A divorce is an emotional event, so it's often hard for the partners to arrive at thoughtful, reasonable decisions. Lawyers can help make these decisions without letting feelings get in the way.

Lawyers can also plan for future events that the couple hadn't thought about. For example, what will happen to the children if one partner moves to another state? By raising such questions ahead of time—and helping to settle them—lawyers can prevent a lot of trouble later on.

Finally, lawyers can help with the technical aspects of a divorce. They can file any necessary legal documents and, if a trial is necessary, represent the partners in court.

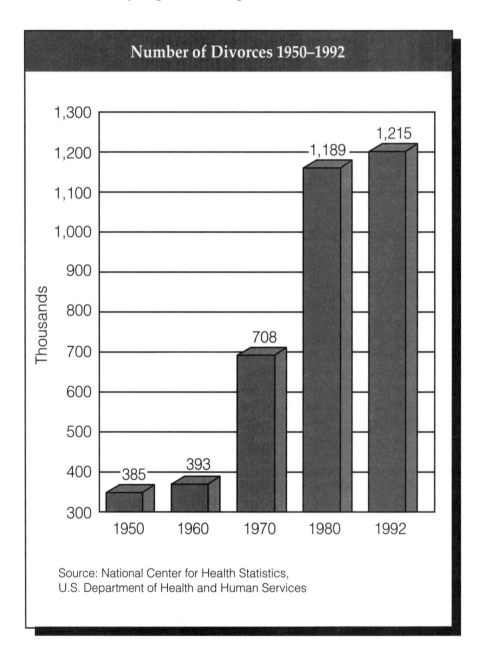

Number of Divorces 1950–1992

Source: National Center for Health Statistics,
U.S. Department of Health and Human Services

Mediation

Hiring lawyers sometimes makes it harder, rather than easier, for a couple to reach an agreement. Each lawyer tries to "win" as much as possible for the partner he or she is representing. If neither lawyer is willing to back down, the divorce may drag on for a very long time. In the meantime, the relationship between the divorcing partners gets worse.

For this reason, the judge in a contested divorce will sometimes recommend that the couple hire a mediator. The mediator's job is to help the couple reach an agreement that is fair to both partners.

Unlike a lawyer, a mediator doesn't take sides. Instead, he or she tries to look at the "big picture" to figure out what arrangement will best fit the needs of the divorcing couple and their children. A mediator may talk separately with the wife and the husband, and then talk with both together. He or she may suggest compromises or alternatives that the partners hadn't thought of. With the help of a good mediator, a couple can settle their divorce quickly and with much less anger.

For example, Karl and Vivian agreed that their three children should live with Vivian after their divorce. But Karl didn't want Vivian to have the family house. The house had belonged to Karl's parents, and before that to his grandparents. Karl thought that he should get to keep the house and that Vivian and the children should find another place to live. Vivian thought that she should get to keep the house, so that the children's lives would be disrupted as little as possible. Neither Karl nor Vivian was willing to give in.

Finally, Karl and Vivian brought in a mediator. The mediator suggested that Vivian be allowed to keep the house temporarily, until all the children were grown. Once the children had moved out, Vivian would have to give the house back to Karl. Karl and Vivian hadn't thought of this possibility. They both agreed to the mediator's suggestion, and their divorce went ahead smoothly.

Finances

When two people marry, they often pool their money and property. Cash and possessions are no longer "mine" and "yours"; they are "ours." The same is true of debts. If a married couple borrows money to buy a house or a car, both partners are responsible for making sure the loan is repaid.

If the couple has children, both partners are responsible for meeting the children's needs. They must make sure the children have food, clothing, shelter, and education.

When a couple divorces, they must divide their money and their property. They must also divide their financial obligations—their responsibility to pay back debts and to care for their children.

Dividing Property

In a contested divorce, the law of each state dictates how a couple's property is to be divided. In most cases, all property and debts are split 50-50. This is true regardless of which partner earned the larger share of the family income.

Of course, this doesn't mean that the couple's car must be cut down the middle. The partners (and their lawyers) can usually work out ways to distribute larger items equally. For example, the partner who has custody of the children will usually keep the house and furniture. The other partner may take the car and a larger portion of the family's savings.

Sometimes, a large item such as a house may be the only valuable thing a family owns. If one partner takes the house, there may be very little left for the other partner to take. In such cases, it is sometimes necessary to sell the house and divide the money between the divorcing partners.

Alimony

Alimony is money paid by one ex-spouse to support the other. In many families, only one partner works to earn money. The other partner stays at home to raise the children or take care of the house. If such a couple splits up, the partner who stays at home may suddenly be left without an income. Because that partner has no recent employment experience, it may be hard for him or her to find a job. If he or she does get hired, it will probably be for a very low-paying position.

Alimony is a way to help even out the income-related inequality. After the divorce, the partner who has the better-paying job makes periodic payments to the other partner. The other partner uses these payments for housing, food, clothing, and other living expenses. Alimony payments continue until the underemployed spouse remarries or begins earning enough money to be self-supporting. And the amount of the payments can be adjusted if circumstances change.

Alimony payments are becoming less common. Today, many judges prefer to make a clean break between divorcing partners. They feel that anyone who remains financially dependent on an ex-spouse is less likely to become independent in the long run.

For this reason, only about 10 percent of recent divorce cases involve alimony payments. If one spouse needs financial support, the judge may give him or her a larger portion of the couple's property at the time of the divorce.

Child Support

The responsibility of parents to care for their children doesn't end at divorce. Both of your parents—even when they're no longer married—are still legally required to take care of you until you're old enough to take care of yourself. Among other things, they must make sure that you have food and clothing, that you have a comfortable place to live, and that you continue to go to school.

Generally, the parent you're living with will have the primary responsibility for your well-being. But the other parent will have to pay part of the cost of taking care of you. He or she will

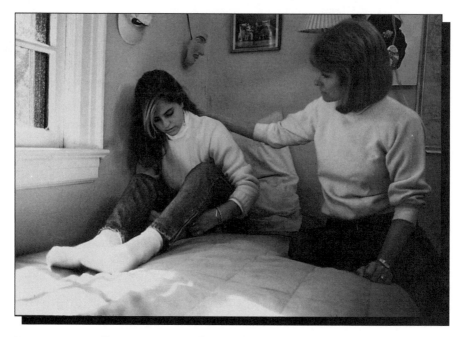

Your parents will want you to understand that, though they will live apart, they still love you. The future may seem scary, but you may be assured that your parents are required by law to take care of you.

do this by making child support payments to the parent you're living with.

The child support payments can be used only for your needs. For example, they can be used to help pay for your food, clothing, medical care, and education. They cannot be used for other family expenses, such as buying living room furniture or a new car.

The amount of each child support payment will be set by the court, depending on what your parent can afford. As with alimony, the amount can be reduced later if the parent loses a job or retires.

In most states, parents are legally required to support their children until they're 18 years old. The payments may end sooner if the child marries or takes a permanent, full-time job.

Some parents agree to support their children for a longer period of time—for example, until they finish college.

Financial Difficulties

Divorce usually causes a strain on family finances. Your parents must now support two households instead of one. The
parent you live with may need to get a job—or a second job—
to be able to meet the extra expenses. So you may find that you
have added responsibilities, such as housecleaning, cooking, or
babysitting.

To make things worse, it's possible that your other parent
will fall behind in alimony or child support payments. You
may have to deal with the difficulties of living on only one parent's income.

When a parent fails to make child support payments, his or
her children often take it personally. They may see the lack of
payments as a sign that the parent doesn't love them. But it's
much more likely that the parent is having a difficult time
financially and can't afford to make the payments.

Sometimes, one parent withholds child support in order to
get back at the other parent. He or she may not realize that it's
really the children who will suffer from this behavior.

In any case, no parent has the right to stop paying child support without court permission. State laws are making it harder
and harder for parents to avoid their financial responsibility. If
a parent stops making payments, his or her employer may be
required to take the required amount out of the parent's pay-
check every month.

Once the divorce process begins, it may seem like it will never
end. But the laws of every state and the courts that enforce those
laws make sure that the process does end eventually.

Interview

Now that she's in her twenties, Sandi says that some memories of her parents' divorce are as clear as if they happened yesterday. Other memories of those days are gone forever. She does know that the divorce, for a number of reasons, made her grow up faster. Sandi's story brings up many of the problems facing teens whose parents are divorcing.

Mom was 19 and Dad was 26 when they met. They married after knowing each other for six weeks.

My mom had just broken up with her high school sweetheart, the man she thought she was going to marry. My dad had just moved to the area; it was his first time away from his folks. He was at a point where his career was starting off, and he wanted a family and a wife at home to take care of him.

There were two of us kids, me and my sister, Alison, who is about five years younger. My father is an electrical engineer. My mother taught dance classes to children during the day, and at night she taught adult social dancing—ballroom dancing, disco dancing.

When I was a teenager, my mother insisted that I help her out with her classes, because she'd need a partner, so I went to a lot of these dance classes with her. At the same time, my dad was pushing for me to take math classes. I wasn't in the college track in math, and he felt that I could be. So here I was in summer school taking algebra, and I can remember my mom insisting that I go to classes with her, and I'd be freaking out because I had to do homework for algebra. Needless to say, I felt a great deal of pressure.

If I were to marry and have a child, I think I'd be more of a team player with my husband, and together we would have some ideas and some coordination about what we wanted for our child and perhaps check in with the *child* every so often and get some feedback. I remember as a child just not feeling like I had any choice, that I had to fulfill the expectations of my parents.

My parents divorced when I was 16. My mother told me the news. She told me that she and my father were getting a divorce and that she was moving out. I don't remember too much more about that day. I don't remember my father or Alison being there. We didn't have any family meeting or anything.

I would say that I wasn't very surprised about the divorce. I wasn't too upset about the news initially, but then my life changed. I had to deal with the shared holidays issue—celebrating Christmas twice, celebrating Thanksgiving twice. I still live that way. I just celebrated my birthday, and, like always, I've got these different family factions I've got to please.

My parents talked to me all the time about their financial worries. I was under the impression that there was no money whatsoever. I was told that our house would have to be sold. That was very disturbing to me. I didn't want to give up the house where I'd grown up.

And they talked about each other to me. They would each build a case against the other of why they were the victim and why the other parent was bad to them or mean to them or why it was the other parent's fault that they were divorcing.

I found myself feeling that I constantly had to defend the other parent from the criticism, so I'd be with one parent and they'd say something, and I'd have to say, "Oh, no, that's not the case." They really played on my sympathy and emotions.

At one point, my mom's lawyer asked me which parent would I choose to live with. They asked my sister—my sister was 10 at the time, and she's being asked, "Which parent? Choose a parent." Our loyalties were questioned. Worse than that, our security was threatened, because we were told we didn't have money, and it was all because of the divorce.

We ended up living with our father at first. Very early on, my sister expressed a lot of anger toward my mom. If it was time to go over to Mom's to celebrate, she was always complaining she didn't want to go. I felt that I was always in the role of the peacekeeper: "Oh, come on, it's not that bad, come on let's go." But I was also feeling that a guilt trip was being laid on us. My mom was saying, "You have to spend the holiday with me; otherwise, I'm so alone, and don't you love me?"

I lived with my dad during college. After graduation from college, it was very difficult for me to move away from my father's house, because I was afraid that my dad wouldn't have a social life. He seemed very dependent on having me in the house; otherwise, he was lonely. I was very involved in my parents' lives.

Soon after the divorce, my dad met a woman. He met her on a business trip; they had this whirlwind romance. They got married during a business trip to Hawaii, and this woman arrived with her kids. She stayed for about six months. In that time, Alison's life and my life were very disrupted by this woman we didn't have any rapport with. Her kids weren't very well-behaved. There was a lot of chaos and shouting, and my father was always tired and harried, and it was just ugly. Finally, she just moved out.

My mom was desperate. She talked about wanting to be married. She'd tell me she was afraid of growing old and being alone. She'd broken up with the boyfriend she'd been living with—she decided he had been abusive and he wasn't really going to marry her.

She began a marathon of dates with different men. I was very disturbed that she was so needy. I felt very bad for her. I wanted to be protective. I was relieved when she finally met the man she's married to now. I thought, "Oh thank goodness; she's finally married someone, and she'll be happy."

Mom says that if she had known what she was in for, she would perhaps not have divorced my father, but at the time she was very naïve. If she had seen a better therapist who'd had some more creative ideas on how she could deal with the dissatisfaction she felt in her life, perhaps she might not have divorced, or might not have divorced at that time.

It certainly has made me very cautious about the kind of person I want to marry. I'm very focused on what I want to do and how I want to live my life. So being in a relationship is not a priority for me. It's been a really strong priority for my parents—both my parents—and they seem to have made frantic, desperate choices in whom they've paired up with, because what was important to them was not the person so much as just being in the relationship.

Me, well I'm still trying to figure out how I really feel about marriage.

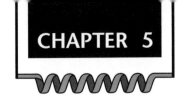

CHAPTER 5

Where Do You Fit In?

Q My parents are splitting up. What's going to happen to my sister and me? Can we stay together? Which of our parents will I live with? Will I ever get to see the parent I'm not living with?

A The answers to most of these questions are up to your parents. As part of their divorce settlement, your parents will have to reach an agreement about where their children will live. They'll have to figure out what makes the best sense for you and for them.

• • • • • • • • • • • •

Their decision will be based partly on practical considerations. For example, which of your parents will have the bigger house? Which will live closer to your school? Which will have more time to spend with you?

But the decision will also be based on feelings. For example, which of your parents do you have a closer relationship with? How would you feel about having two homes—that is, living part-time with one parent and part-time with the other?

Most divorcing couples say that decisions about the children are the most difficult for them to make. You can count on your parents to put a lot of careful thought into these questions. They will undoubtedly spend a lot of time talking—to each other and to you—before they come to a final decision.

Whatever that decision turns out to be, remember that both your parents still care about you. It may not seem that way at the time. Your parents may decide, for instance, that you and your sister should live with your mother. This doesn't mean your father has stopped loving you. It means he loves you so much that he's willing to make a great sacrifice. In order to make sure you have the best life possible, he's willing to set aside his desire to live with you.

If you do end up living with just one parent, you'll almost certainly get to spend time with the other parent. The new arrangements may take time to get used to, but as time passes, you may find that you've grown closer to both of your parents.

Types of Custody

There are no set rules about where children should live when their parents break up. Every child is an individual and has individual needs. It is clear, however, that every child needs someone to depend on—not just for food and shelter, but for making serious decisions. For example, someone needs to decide what sort of education and religious training you're going to get. If you become ill, someone has to decide which doctor to take you to and what medical advice to follow.

When parents get divorced, a judge gives custody of the children to one parent, both parents, or a third person. Custody is the right to live with the child and to make important decisions about the child's life.

Sole Custody

Years ago, when a couple got divorced, the children were almost always sent to live with the mother. In legal terms, the mother had sole custody of the children—that is, she was completely responsible for taking care of them. Every week or so, the children would spend a day with their father, and occasionally they would be allowed to stay with him overnight. The father was required to pay his share of child support. But other than that, he had a very small role in his children's lives.

Today, sole custody is much less common. Most divorced parents share custody of their children. There are still some situations, however, in which one parent (not necessarily the mother) may be granted sole custody.

Sometimes, the two parents live so far apart that it would be hard for the children to travel back and forth between them. Sometimes, one parent is clearly not fit for parenthood—for example, he or she may have a history of abusing or neglecting the children.

More often, however, the problem is simply a matter of communication. Sharing custody requires that the divorced parents be able to cooperate with each other. They must be able to agree on major decisions concerning the children. They must

These sisters want to stay together after their parents are divorced. Their parents will take their feelings into consideration when making a decision about living arrangements.

also be able to coordinate the children's travel between two different homes. If the parents are so angry at each other that they can't deal with these issues, a judge may grant custody to only one of them.

Sometimes, it's the parents—not the court—who choose sole custody. Some parents feel strongly that it's important for children to have a single, stable home, even if that means living with just one parent. They believe that having to go back and forth between two homes would disrupt their children's lives. For these reasons, one of the parents may decide to give the other parent sole custody.

Joint Custody
May's parents live six blocks away from each other. May has a bedroom and clothing in each house. She spends a week living in her father's house, then a week at her mother's. Because her parents live so close together, May can go to the same school and visit the same friends no matter which house she's in.

May's parents have an agreement called joint custody. (It's sometimes also known as divided custody or shared custody.) Because it gives children a chance to grow up with both parents, joint custody is the preferred arrangement today.

There are many ways to handle joint custody. Children may spend half a week with one parent and half a week with the other, or as much as a year with one parent and a year with the other. Some children spend the school year with one parent and summer vacations with the other. In most cases, decisions about minor issues—such as curfew and household chores— are made by whichever parent the children are with at the time. Both parents decide together on the bigger issues.

Split Custody
Sometimes, parents with two or more children agree to a split custody arrangement; that is, they divide the children between them. Each parent then has sole custody of at least one child.

While it's often best for brothers and sisters to stay together, sometimes it makes more sense for them not to. For example, a girl might prefer to live with her mother, while her brothers would rather be with their father. Or the younger children might be more comfortable in the neighborhood they're familiar with, while the older children would be better off in another town with a better high school.

Living Arrangements of Children, 1970–1991

| | | Percent Living With | | |
Race, Hispanic Origin, and Year	Number (thousands)	Both Parents	Mother Only	Father Only
White				
1970	58,790	90	8	1
1980	52,242	83	14	2
1991	51,918	79	17	3
African American				
1970	9,422	59	30	2
1980	9,375	42	44	2
1991	10,209	36	54	4
Hispanic+				
1970	4,006	78	NA	NA
1980	5,459	75	20	2
1991	7,462	66	27	3

NA = Not available
+ = Hispanic persons may be of any race.
Source: Bureau of the Census

You'll be able to share time with both parents after a divorce. For example, if you're living with your mom during the week, you may have the fun of visiting your father on the weekend.

Third-Party Custody

Very rarely, neither parent is able—or willing—to take responsibility for the children. In those cases, the children may be allowed to live with someone who isn't their parent, perhaps a relative or a close family friend. This arrangement is called third-party custody.

Even if one or both parents want custody of their children, third-party custody is sometimes a better idea. For example, it's sometimes better for children to stay in their old school, even if both their parents choose to move away from the area. In this case, they might be allowed to stay with an adult who lives closer to the school. This way the children do not have to adjust to a new school, new teachers, and new friends all at the same time.

Parents whose children are in third-party custody continue to act as parents. They see their children regularly and continue to support them financially.

Who Decides

Although divorce is difficult for any couple, it is even more painful for a couple with children. Even if your parents no longer love each other or simply cannot reconcile differences happily enough to stay with each other, they still love their children. They want to share in your life and the lives of your sisters and brothers as much as possible. For this reason, coming up with a custody arrangement that satisfies both your parents may be nearly impossible.

If your parents can't come to an acceptable decision, a judge may have to make the decision for them. The judge will try to figure out which arrangement is in your best interest.

The judge may enlist the help of a social worker before making a decision. The social worker will meet with you, your brothers or sisters, and each of your parents. After finding out what your living situations are like, the social worker will submit a report to the judge. Based on that report, the judge will decide what custody arrangement is best.

Your Wishes

Because your parents' divorce settlement will affect your entire life, your feelings are very important. Before they make a custody decision, your parents or the judge will probably ask you what you want.

For most children, deciding which parent to live with seems nearly impossible. Most children love both their parents. They feel as if they're being asked to take sides, or to choose a favorite between the two people they love the most.

Even when children *do* know which parent they'd rather live with, they may be afraid to say so. They don't want to speak honestly if it means hurting either parent's feelings.

Of course, the judge or your parents may not necessarily choose the custody arrangement you want. If this happens, keep in mind that they're doing what they believe is best for you. The arrangement a child or young person wants may not always be possible or practical.

Visitation

If you are to live with one parent, the other parent will most likely be given the right to visitation—that is, a chance to spend time with you away from the parent you live with.

Most young people find parental visits awkward, especially at first. Parents, eager to spend quality time with their children, sometimes take them to special events, movies, or all-day activities. Many children soon realize that what's really important is not doing something special with their parent, but just spending time together. They often find that doing routine, ordinary things like washing the car, working on a school project, preparing a special meal, or shopping can be fun. These activities give the child and the parent a time to talk, catch up on what's going on, and keep in touch with each other's lives.

Visitation is an important time for both the children and the parent. It's important to try to stay close to both parents, even if you see them infrequently, or if they live far away.

Making It Work

Child custody arrangements can be difficult, especially at first. Parents who aren't getting along may be unwilling to deal with the problems of moving their children back and forth between two different homes. They may also have trouble making important decisions about their children's lives.

Some divorced parents take out their anger at each other through their children. They "accidentally" miss the scheduled meeting time, so that their child misses a visit with the other parent. Or they move to a distant city and take the children along, making it difficult for the other parent to see the children. In response, some frustrated parents have kidnapped their own children.

All of these actions make things worse, not better. They make it hard for the family—especially the children—to settle into a new way of life. They may also be against the law. If either parent has violated the divorce agreement, his or her ex-spouse can take that parent to court. A judge may then take away some or all of the parent's custody or visitation rights.

No matter how fair a custody arrangement may be, getting used to it always takes time. You, your parents, and other members of your family may be unhappy or uneasy for a while. But as time passes, the new way of life will become more familiar.

CHAPTER 6

Settling In

 Q I see my dad every Saturday. I love him, but I'm starting to hate getting together. He always feels he has to take me someplace or buy me something. We can never just relax together, the way we did in the old days. What should I do?

 A A lot of teens have the same complaint about visitation. They say things are too formal. They say that it's like spending time with some distant relative, not like seeing a parent.

• • • • • • • • • • • •

Before your parents divorced, you and your dad probably spent time doing ordinary things—working around the house, or doing homework together. There are many possible reasons why this is no longer true.

Since you and your dad only get together once a week, he probably wants to make sure that your time together is fun and memorable. He may think you'd be unhappy just sitting around with him.

He also wants to keep you from feeling deprived because of the divorce. He may feel guilty about the divorce; he knows it hurts you to have to see him by appointment. Maybe he's buying you things to make up for that. Or maybe he feels that he's competing with your mother to be "best parent," and he's buying you things to win that competition.

In any case, he probably doesn't even realize that you are

uncomfortable with the way he's treating you. The best thing you can do is to let him know. If you and your dad used to cook dinner together, why not suggest that you do that the next time you get together? In the same way, you might ask your dad to help you with a school project, or with softball or band practice. Doing these things will make your times together more like they were before the divorce.

If your father feels guilty about not "doing anything" during your visits, assure him that this is what you want. Maybe you can come to a compromise—do something special once a month or so, and on the rest of the visits do ordinary activities.

Getting Used to Things

When your parents divorce, your life will be different in many ways. For one thing, you probably won't see either parent as much as you're used to. Even if you live with one parent full-time, you're likely to see that parent less. He or she will probably have to go to work. In time, he or she may develop a more active social life and may begin dating. And you'll be out of the house more, spending time with your friends and the other parent.

Your parents probably told you that things at home would be calmer after the divorce. While this is true, it may not be true immediately. There are lots of things to work out first. You may see lots of arguing as your parents go through the legal or financial issues of the divorce. During this time, they're likely to be upset, worried, and angry. Your relationships with them may not be as easy as they used to be, but it's important that you keep lines of communication open at all times.

You may have some practical adjustments to make, as well, such as getting used to a new home or a new school. Most children of divorced parents say the first two years are the hardest. After that, routines get established and everyone's life begins to feel more normal.

How Parents Adjust

Immediately after a divorce, your parents may begin to act in ways that make you uncomfortable. This is understandable—if the divorce is strange and difficult for you, imagine how it is for them. As they begin to put together a new life, they may go through some of the same stages of adjustment that you're going through.

Like you, your parents will be dealing with a mixture of many different feelings. They may feel like failures after the divorce. It's common for divorcing parents to feel that they've failed to live up to everyone's expectations—their own, their children's, and society's. They may feel that they've lost the love and respect of everyone they know, including you.

Your parents will probably also feel guilty. They know that the divorce made you unhappy, and they know they're responsible for making you feel that way. At the same time, they may feel angry at each other and bitter about the breakup. A divorcing parent is also likely to be worried about everyone's future—his or her own, yours, and that of the other parent.

On top of everything else, parents who divorce are suffering because it is the end of a relationship. As always happens when someone loses a partner, your parents are likely to feel depressed and lonely. Unless each of them is in a relationship with someone else, they must do by themselves the things they once did as a pair. Their social lives may change dramatically. Often, divorcing couples end up dividing up the friends they have in common. In some cases, one partner can lose those friendships entirely.

Rachel's mother became extremely dependent on her during the first year after the divorce. Not only did she expect Rachel to do extra chores, but she also relied on Rachel as a confidante and friend. At first, she shared with Rachel the kinds of things she used to share with her husband—for example, stories about coworkers and problems at the office. Rachel didn't

mind listening to her mother, although she didn't really understand most of the stories. In time, Rachel's mother began
sharing her worries about finances and gossip about other family members. When she began dating, she would fill Rachel in
on details of the date. Rachel knew her mother needed a friend
to talk to, but she didn't really like her new position. She felt
that she had gained a girlfriend, but she'd lost a mother.

Competition for Affection

After a divorce, most parents feel a strong need for affection,
especially from their children. They want to be reassured that
their children still love them and that they don't hold the
divorce against them. Unfortunately, this need drives some
divorced parents to compete against each other for their children's affection. Many children have said that this is the
hardest part of life after a divorce.

"Good Parent/Bad Parent"

Some parents compete for affection by trying to poison the
children's minds against the other parent. Melissa's father was
like that. Every time Melissa went to visit her father, he would
say nasty things about her mother: "You know, Melissa, this
whole divorce was her fault. Did you know she slept with a
guy while I was away on business? Did she ever tell you that?"
Melissa hated hearing these things about her mother. She
didn't care if what her father was saying was true; she just
didn't want to hear it. She grew to dislike visiting her father
because of his comments.

The best way to handle it when one parent says bad things
about the other is to put a stop to it. Tell the parent that you
don't want to hear about their differences. If stating your feelings directly doesn't put an end to the remarks, simply walk
away whenever your parent starts to make them. Maybe then
he or she will understand what a difficult position you're in.

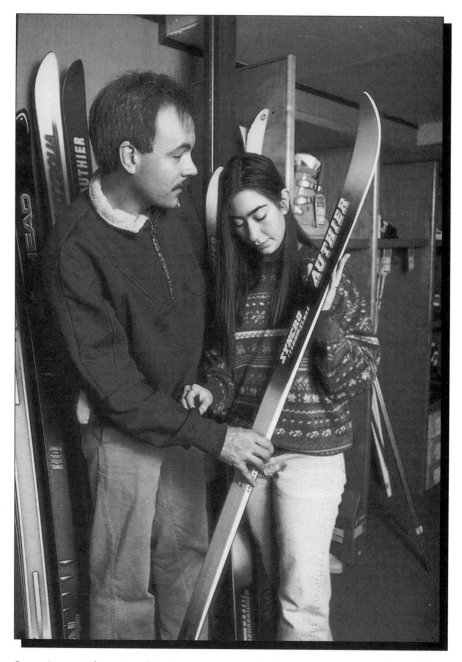

Sometimes, either out of guilt or a need to make up for his or her absence, a visiting parent goes overboard to impress a child with expensive gifts or entertainment. It's not always the best way to spend time together.

Competition Through Bribery

Your parents may compete with each other by trying to treat you better than the other parent does. They may give you things that they know you want. They may permit you to do things that the other parent won't permit. They may relax rules around the house when you visit.

For example, Pearl lived with her father. She only saw her mother every other weekend. At her father's house, Pearl was required to prepare dinner and help with the laundry. At her mother's house, she had no duties. Her mother never disciplined her. She always took Pearl on exciting adventures and treated her to fancy meals. At first, Pearl thought of her mother as her favorite. In time, she began to realize that she was being unfair. Her father was the one who was raising her. It was easy for her mother to be the fun parent when they only got together a couple of times a month. Pearl learned to respect her father for the hard work he did in raising her and stopped viewing either one as a favorite.

Like Pearl, most children are not fooled for long by special treatment. As much as they enjoy the gifts and lack of discipline, most wise up and see these things for what they are: bribery. Eventually, they may become uncomfortable with the attention and begin to resent it.

Your Parents' Relationship with Each Other

Some couples remain friends after the divorce. They see each other socially, they have no trouble working out the custody and visitation agreements, and they sincerely want the best for each other. But this is not true for all couples. Many remain resentful or angry for years. Others simply cannot get along with each other.

Jealousy is the most common obstacle to friendships between ex-spouses. Either of your parents may be jealous of the other for a number of reasons. One may feel that the other got the better deal in the divorce settlement. One may feel that the other has a better relationship with the children. One may be jealous when the other begins a new romantic relationship.

When there are bad feelings between parents, the children too often get caught in the middle. Some parents deliberately use their children to get back at each other.

Sending Messages

Divorced parents often send messages to each other through their children. Sometimes, these messages are simple and straightforward: "Tell your father I'll pick you up at six o'clock," or "Remind your mother about your recital next week." Other messages are less straightforward and are intended more for *you* to hear: "Tell your mother that if she loved you, she wouldn't be late picking you up every week," or "Tell your father that if he spent less money on alcohol, you could have a new bike." These aren't real messages; they're just ways in which parents bad-mouth each other in front of the children. If either of your parents does this, you should make it clear that you don't want to be caught in the middle of their disagreements. Tell them you won't deliver such messages.

Spying

Often, parents like to keep tabs on each other. Each wants to know as much as possible about the other: how they are feel-ing, whether they are dating, and whether they are surviving the divorce. If they're not on good terms with each other, the best way to find out this information is through the children.

Many children who return to one parent after visiting with the other find themselves being grilled for information. For example, your mother may ask, "Does Dad have a girlfriend?" or "Did he say anything about me?" A parent may even ask you to spy at the other's house to satisfy his or her need to know how the other is doing.

The best thing you can do in these situations is to stay out of it. Refuse to answer the questions. Tell them that you want to have honest relationships with both parents, and being used as a spy ruins your chances to do so.

Outright Battles

Unless one of your parents has no visitation rights, your parents are going to have to keep in touch with each other. They may have to arrange to pick you up at each other's home. They may both want to attend special events such as school recitals, birthday parties, or graduation. Some parents simply can't be civil when they see their ex-spouses. They fight or refuse to speak. This can make things awkward for you. It may even ruin your special occasions.

Ask your parents to behave for your sake when they're together. If they aren't able to do so, you might arrange for them not to have to see each other at all; for example, have them pick you up at school or at neighbors' houses. If they can't be polite to each other at graduation or other events, ask them not to attend.

Talking to Your Parents

After her divorce, Nathan's mother constantly complained about how her husband had mistreated her. Nathan hated hearing about it. He knew he should tell her to stop, but he didn't want to. His mother was already hurting, and Nathan didn't want to make her feel worse. He wanted to protect her from feeling that she was a bad parent.

Like Nathan, many children find it hard to speak to their divorced parents about how they feel. If you're in that situation, you might start by talking with someone else. A counselor or adult relative may be able to put your mind at rest.

In some cases, even if you're eager to talk to your parents about your feelings, your parents may not be ready to talk to you. They know the divorce has hurt you, and they may feel guilty, but they may not be prepared to deal with those guilty feelings. Therefore, one or both of your parents may resist talking with you about the divorce. They may seem distant or angry, or they may just quickly change the subject. But even if your parents resist talking with you, it's very important that you continue to try. It can only benefit the situation.

Helping Your Parents

Most of your life, your parents have been there to help you. When you were sad, they comforted you. When you were lonely, they gave you a hug. Now, however, things may be a little different. Right now, it might be your parents who need the comfort and the hugs.

One very important way to help your parents get through the rough times is to show them that you need them. About six months after Yolanda's parents divorced, Yolanda got a part in the school play. She was having trouble learning her lines. Although she knew her mother was preoccupied with her own problems, Yolanda really needed her help. It turned out that

Divorced parents need to consult often about their children. However, many parents find it hard to adjust to their new relationship—communication may be difficult for a while. Children should try their best to be understanding.

asking for her mother's help was the best thing she could have done. It gave her mother something to take her mind off the divorce, at least for a while. It also reminded her how important she was to her daughter.

A Healthier Place

If you look around you, you may see that many of your friends live with one parent, have stepparents, or move back and forth between two homes. Talking with them about their experiences may help you settle more easily into your new life.

If you have trouble making the adjustment, take some time to remember why your parents divorced. Both children and parents tend to glamorize the past. When they think back to earlier times, they tend to remember only the happy times: special occasions, family vacations, and other moments during which everyone got along. They forget a lot of the anger and fighting that went on. It's important to keep realistic memories about the past: there were good times, and there were bad times. If you glamorize the past, you'll have a hard time putting it behind you.

CHAPTER 7

Remarriage and New Families

 My dad's getting remarried. I feel really strange about his new wife moving in with us. I'm happy for Dad, but she's not my mother. How should I treat her?

 It's an odd position to be in. A woman who is not your mother is becoming part of your family. It's natural that you'd feel uncomfortable with her and uncomfortable about the situation.

• • • • • • • • • • • •

Of course she's not your mother. No one expects her to replace your mother. No one expects you to develop exactly the same relationship with your father's new wife as you have with your mother. No one expects you to love her the first time you meet.

What *is* expected of you is that you treat her with courtesy. Your father's new wife is moving into your home. As an adult member of your household, she deserves both your respect and your trust. Remember, she's in a tough position, too. Imagine how it must feel to move into someone's house and settle into a family that's already established. Welcome her to your home, spend time with her, and give her and your father some time alone.

Both of you should expect that it will take time to get to know each other. A good way to start is by spending some time together. Are there any interests that you have in common? Perhaps your father's new wife likes bicycling as much as you do, or perhaps both of you play musical instruments and could practice a few duets.

In time, you and your father's wife should be able to develop some sort of relationship. It may be a parent-child relationship, or it may be more like a friendship. The only way to find out is to give her a chance.

Dating

It can be strange to think of your parents dating and falling in love with other people. But sooner or later they probably will want to meet someone new. Everyone needs companionship and love. You probably hope to find someone special, so it shouldn't be too hard to think of your parents wanting the same for themselves. Would you really rather that your parents spend the rest of their lives lonely and without a partner? Chances are, that would worry you just as much.

However, when your parents begin dating, you may find that you feel a little funny about it. It's strange to think of either of your parents getting involved with someone other than each other.

Some children become jealous when their parents start dating or getting serious about someone. They find that their parents have less time to share with them. The parents may bring their new friends along on visits or invite them home for dinner with the family. If you think of visitation or dinnertime as your time alone together, you may resent having a new person there.

Another problem children of divorced parents may face is that they get attached to their parents' companions. Then they feel bad or resentful if the relationship doesn't work out.

Ann's father dated Helena for over a year. Ann had become very attached to Helena. They were like girlfriends. They

Remarriage may bring unexpected rewards into your life as well as into your parent's. Your parent may at last be happy again, and you may find you have a new friend.

would make dinner together. Sometimes, Helena would spend an entire evening braiding Ann's hair. After a year, Ann's father and Helena broke up. Ann was devastated. She resented every other girlfriend her father brought home.

It's best not to focus too much on your parents' social lives. Like you, your parents will probably want to date a lot before finding someone to settle down with.

A New Spouse

Children of divorced parents often find that a parent's remarriage has bad points and good points. It can take time to get used to the new family member, especially if you haven't spent much time together before the marriage. And it will definitely take time to get used to the new family dynamic, with two adults in the house. But, once you all settle in, you may find that you really like having the additional person around.

Getting Used to It

Artie felt extremely uncomfortable with his father's new wife, Diana. Artie and his father had lived alone together for three years before she moved into their home. They had settled into a routine that Artie found comfortable and comforting. When Diana moved in, Artie saw her as an intrusion on their routine. She had different ways of doing things.

To make his feelings clear, Artie refused to acknowledge Diana. He'd "forget" to set the dinner table for the third person. He'd make a point to direct his conversation to his father and exclude her. In her presence, he would talk about the past and all the things the two of them used to do together.

Doing this only made things more tense. It made everyone unhappy. It didn't make Diana go away, as Artie secretly hoped it would. Instead, it pulled him and his father apart.

A new person in the house needs to find a way to fit in, and those who live there already need to find room for that person.

Make an effort to include the new spouse in your life. If the two of you can't become the best of friends, at least you can work out a good cooperative arrangement so the family can live together in peace.

At the same time, be realistic about what to expect. No person is perfect. You can expect to have conflicts, misunderstandings, and moments when you wish things were different. If you're honest with yourself, you know that things were never perfect between you and your parents, either.

Life with a New Person
If you give the new spouse a chance, you may find that he or she adds a lot to your life. The new adult may take over a few chores and responsibilities that you and your one parent had to handle alone. If the new spouse earns an income, you may be more secure financially. Your newly married parent will be happier now that he or she has found a companion. And, for

When new family members can work things out together, everybody wins.

you, a second adult may offer resources that you never had access to before.

In addition to talents or skills, the new person in your family may prove to be a valuable friend. Many young people find that they can talk to their parents' spouses more easily than they can their parents. Sometimes, it's easier to talk about dating or other serious problems with someone who can be a little more objective than a parent.

New Brothers and Sisters

If your parent's new spouse has children, you may find yourself with instant brothers and sisters. Whether you move into their home or they move into yours, getting used to each other may take some time. Just as with the new adult, you have to find a way to make space in your life for new siblings.

First, of course, there's the problem of finding physical space for everyone. You may need to share a bedroom; you'll undoubtedly have to share bathrooms, the television, and family chores.

You'll also need to find emotional space for each other. Some young people find themselves becoming jealous of new siblings. They become upset when they see their own mothers "mothering" someone else. They are jealous of the time the parent spends with the other children.

It's going to be difficult to overcome some of those feelings. But if you can, the rewards can be great. You'll have the opportunity to have the big brother or the little sister that you have always wanted.

Your Other Parent

Many young people find it hard to welcome a parent's new spouse because they feel that it's somehow disloyal to their other parent. If you feel that pressure, keep in mind that loving someone new doesn't mean you don't also love the other person. You are quite capable of loving both people.

A New Family

It'll take time, patience, and effort to make the new family work. If you keep at it, though, and you are fair to the new members of your family, things will probably work out. Most children in blended families find that they do adjust in time.

Of course, things will never be perfect. You can expect to have the same disagreements and fights that other families have. But you may also develop the same strong family bonds that other families have. If you are able to adjust, you may end up in the enviable position of having a strong family and parents who are much happier than they were when they were together. And, in the end, that's what's best for everyone.

Where to Go for Help

There are a number of national organizations that can help you learn more about parental divorce. Each of these places can get you in touch with a counselor or other person who can answer your questions and send you booklets, brochures, and other information about what you're going through.

Your best bet is to get in touch with the local office of these national organizations. Local groups can get you the help you need right away. To find groups other than the ones listed below, look in your telephone book under "Children's Protective Services," "Family Services," or "Mental Health."

Also, you may want to contact the local offices of the following organizations to see if they have any organized groups for you to consider joining:

Young Men's Christian Association (YMCA)
Young Women's Christian Association (YWCA)
Young Men's Hebrew Association (YMHA)
Young Women's Hebrew Association (YWHA)
Boy's Club of America
Girl's Club of America
Big Brothers/Big Sisters of America

You may also want to contact the local office of Parents Without Partners. This group can be a good resource for your parents as they go through the divorce and also afterward, as they begin their new lives.

Hot Lines

Community Information and
  Referral Services
(800) 352-3792

National Runaway Switchboard
(800) 621-4000

The Nineline
(800) 999-9999

Youth Crisis Hotline
(800) 448-4663

Canadian Organizations

Families in Transition
2 Carlton Street, Suite 917
Toronto, ON M5B 1J3
(416) 585-9151

Family Mediation Canada
  (FMC)
123 Woolwich Street, 2nd Floor
Guelph, ON N1H 3V1
(519) 836-7750

Where to Go for Help

Family Service Canada
55 Parkdale Avenue
Ottawa, ON K1Y 1E5
(613) 728-2463

Kids First Parent Association
   Canada
P.O. Box 36032
RPO Lakeview
Calgary, AB T3E 7C6
(403) 289-1440

Kids Help Phone
2 Bloor Street West, #100
P.O. Box 513
Toronto, ON M4W 3E2
(800) 668-6868

For More Information

Books for Young Adults

Brogan, John P., and Ula Maiden. *The Kids' Guide to Divorce.* Ballantine, 1986.

Friedrich, Liz. *Divorce.* Aladdin Books, 1988.

Johnson, Linda Carlson. *Everything You Need to Know About Your Parents' Divorce.* Rosen, 1992.

Kaplan, Leslie S. *Coping with Stepfamilies.* Rosen, 1991.

LeShan, Eda. *What's Going to Happen to Me?* Four Winds Press, 1978.

Murry, Steve, and Randy Smith. *Divorce Recovery for Teenagers.* Zondervan, 1991.

Rofes, Eric E., ed. *The Kids' Book of Divorce.* Lewis Publishing, 1981.

Other Books

Ahrons, Constance R. *Divorced Families: Meeting the Challenge of Divorce and Remarriage.* W. W. Norton, 1989.

DiCanio, Margaret. *The Encyclopedia of Marriage, Divorce, and the Family.* Facts on File, 1989.

Engel, Marjorie. *Divorce Help Sourcebook.* Invisible Ink, 1994.

Krementz, Jill. *How It Feels When Parents Divorce.* Random House, 1988.

Wallerstein, Judith. *Surviving the Breakup.* Basic Books, 1980.

INDEX